Andreas Nikolaus "**Niki**"
Vienna, Austria was a Formula One driver, a 3-time F1 World
Drivers' Champion, winning in 1975, 1977 and 1984, and an
aviation entrepreneur. Niki was the only driver in F1 history to
have been champion for both Ferrari and McLaren, the sport's
two most successful constructors, being widely regarded as one
of the greatest F1 drivers of all time.

As an aviation entrepreneur, he founded and ran 3 airlines:
Lauda Air, Niki, and Lauda, having been a Bombardier Business
Aircraft brand ambassador. He was also a consultant for
Scuderia Ferrari and team manager of the Jaguar Formula One
racing team for two years. Niki then worked as a pundit for
German TV during Grand Prix weekends, having been non-
executive chairman of Mercedes-AMG Petronas Motorsport, of
which Lauda owned 10%.

Having emerged as Formula One's star driver with a title win
during 1975, while leading the following year's championship
battle, Niki was seriously injured in a crash at the German Grand
Prix of 1976 at the Nürburgring, during which his Ferrari 312T2
burst into flames, having come close to death after inhaling hot
toxic fumes and suffering severe burns.

However, Lauda recovered enough to race again just 6 weeks
later at the Italian Grand Prix. Although he narrowly lost the
title to James Hunt that year, he won his 2nd Ferrari crown the
next, during his final season with the team. After a couple of
years at Brabham then a 2 year break, Niki returned to race 4
seasons for McLaren from 1982 to 1985, during which he won
the title of 1984 by half a point, ahead of his teammate Alain
Prost.

Niki Lauda was born into a wealthy family, his paternal grandfather having been the Viennese-born industrialist Hans Lauda, Niki becoming a racing driver despite his family's disapproval. After starting out with a Mini, Lauda moved on into Formula Vee, as was usual in Central Europe, but soon moved up to drive in private Porsche and Chevron sports cars.

As his career had stalled, Niki took out a £30,000 bank loan, secured by a life insurance policy, to buy his way into the fledgling March team as a Formula Two (F2) driver in 1971, having had an ongoing feud with his family over his racing ambitions, abandoning further contact. He was quickly promoted to the F1 team, having driven for March in F1 and F2 during 1972. Although the F2 cars were competitive, with Lauda's driving skills impressing March principal Robin Herd, the team's F1 season was catastrophic.

Perhaps their lowest point of the season came at the Canadian Grand Prix at Mosport Park, where both March cars were disqualified within 3 laps of each other after just over 3/4 of the race distance. Niki took out another bank loan to buy his way into the BRM team in 1973, having been quick, but the team was in decline. His big break came when his BRM teammate Clay Regazzoni left to rejoin Ferrari the following year, team owner Enzo Ferrari asking him what he thought of Lauda, Clay speaking so favourably of him that Enzo promptly signed him, paying Niki enough to clear his debts.

After an unsuccessful start to the '70s culminating in a disastrous beginning to the 1973 season, Ferrari regrouped under Luca di Montezemolo, having been resurgent the following year. The team's faith in the little-known Lauda was soon rewarded with a 2nd-place finish in his first race for them, the season-opening Argentine Grand Prix.

Niki's debut Grand Prix (GP) victory, which was the first for Ferrari since 1972 , followed only 3 races later in the Spanish Grand Prix. Although Lauda became the season's pacesetter, with 6 successive pole positions, a mixture of inexperience and mechanical unreliability led to him winning only one more race that year, the Dutch GP. Niki finished 4th in the Drivers' Championship in 1974, having shown great commitment to testing and improving the car.

The following F1 season started slowly for Lauda, as after no better than a 5th-place finish in the first 4 races, he won 4 of the next 5, driving the new Ferrari 312T. His first World Championship was confirmed with a third-place finish at the Italian Grand Prix at Monza, Niki's teammate Regazzoni winning the race, as Ferrari clinched their first Constructors' Championship for 11 years.

Lauda then picked up a 5th win at the last race of 1975, the United States GP at Watkins Glen. He also became the first driver to lap the Nürburgring Nordschleife in under 7 minutes, which was considered a great feat, the Nordschleife section of the Nürburgring being later shortened by 2 miles. Niki was known for giving away any trophies he won to his local garage, in exchange for his car being washed and serviced.

Despite tensions between Lauda and Montezemolo's successor, Daniele Audetto, he dominated the start of the following F1 season, winning 4 of the first 6 races, having finished 2nd in the other two. By the time of his 5th win of the year at the British GP, he'd more than twice the points of his closest challengers Jody Scheckter and James Hunt, with a 2nd successive World

Championship appearing a formality, which hadn't happened since Jack Brabham's triumphs of 1959 - 1960. Niki also appeared likely to win the most races in a season, a record held by the late Jim Clark since 1963.

A week before the German Grand Prix of 1976 at the Nürburgring, despite being the fastest driver on that circuit, Lauda urged his fellow drivers to boycott the race. This was mainly because of the 14 mile, very long course's safety arrangements, Niki being concerned about the organisers' lack of resources to properly manage it, including lack of fire marshals, fire and safety equipment and safety vehicles. However, most of the other drivers voted against the boycott, so the race went ahead.

On 1st August 1976, during his 2nd lap at the very fast left kink before Bergwerk, Lauda's Ferrari swerved off the track, hit an embankment, bursting into flames, before making contact with Brett Lunger's Surtees-Ford car. Niki was trapped in the wreckage, with drivers Arturo Merzario, Lunger, Guy Edwards, and Harald Ertl soon arriving at the scene, but before Merzario was able to pull Lauda from his car, he suffered severe burns to his head, having inhaled hot toxic gases that damaged his lungs and blood. As Niki was wearing a modified helmet, because it didn't fit him properly, the foam had compressed, so it slid off his head after the accident, leaving his face exposed to the fire. Although Lauda was conscious, having been able to stand straight after the accident, he later lapsed into a coma.

Niki suffered extensive scarring from the burns to his head, losing most of his right ear as well as the hair on the right side of his head, his eyebrows, and his eyelids. He decided to limit reconstructive surgery to replacing his eyelids then getting them to work properly. Following the accident Lauda always wore a cap to cover the scars on his head, sponsors using the cap for advertising. With Niki out of the contest, Carlos Reutemann was taken on as his replacement but Ferrari boycotted the Austrian Grand Prix, in protest at what they believed was preferential treatment of McLaren driver James Hunt at the Spanish and British Grands Prix.

Lauda missed only two races, appearing at the Monza press conference 6 weeks after the accident with his fresh burns still bandaged, finishing 4th in the Italian GP, despite being petrified. F1 journalist Nigel Roebuck recalled seeing Niki in the pits, peeling the blood-soaked bandages off his scarred scalp, having had to wear a specially adapted crash helmet to reduce his discomfort.

In Lauda's absence, Hunt had mounted a late charge to reduce Niki's lead in the World Championship standings. James and Lauda were friends away from the circuit, with their personal on-track rivalry, while intense, being cleanly contested and fair. After wins at the Canadian and United States Grands Prix, Hunt was only 3 points behind Niki before the final race of the season, the Japanese Grand Prix.

Lauda qualified in third, a place behind Hunt, but on race day there was torrential rain, Niki retiring after two laps, later having said that he felt it was unsafe to continue under the conditions, as his eyes were watering excessively, because of his fire-damaged tear ducts and inability to blink. James led for much of the race before his tyres blistered, a pit stop dropping him down the order but recovered to third, to lift the title by a single point.

Lauda's previously good relationship with Ferrari was severely damaged by his decision to withdraw from the Japanese Grand Prix, having had a troubled season during 1977, despite easily winning the championship by being consistent rather than the fastest. Niki didn't like his new teammate, Carlos Reutemann, who'd been his replacement driver, Lauda being uncomfortable with the move, feeling that he'd been let down by Ferrari:

"We never could stand each other, and instead of taking pressure off me, they put on even more by bringing Carlos Reutemann into the team." Having announced his decision to quit Ferrari at the end of the season, Niki left earlier, after he won the Drivers' Championship at the United States Grand Prix, because of the team's decision to run the unknown Gilles Villeneuve in a third car at the Canadian Grand Prix.

Having joined Parmalat-sponsored Brabham-Alfa Romeo in 1978 for a $1 million salary, Lauda had two unsuccessful seasons, best remembered for his race in the Brabham BT46B, a radical design known as the Fan Car, which won its first and only race at the Swedish GP, but Brabham didn't use the car in F1 again. Other teams strongly protested against the Fan Car's legality, Brabham team owner Bernie Ecclestone then maneuvering for acquisition of Formula One's commercial rights, not wanting to fight a long battle over the car, but the victory in Sweden remained official.

The Brabham BT46 Alfa Romeo flat-12 began that year's season at the third race in South Africa, having suffered from a variety of troubles that forced Niki to retire the car in 9 out of 14 races. Lauda's best results, other than the wins in Sweden and Italy after the penalization of Mario Andretti and Gilles Villeneuve, were 2nd in Montreal and Great Britain, with a 3rd in the Netherlands.

As the Alfa flat-12 engine was too wide for effective wing cars designs, Alfa provided a V12 for 1979, the 4th 12-cylinder engine design that Niki had driven in F1 since 1973. Lauda's season was again marred by retirements and poor speed, even though he won the non-championship Dino Ferrari Grand Prix with the Brabham-Alfa that year. In the single make BMW M1 Procar Championship, driving for the British Formula Two team Project Four Racing, led by Ron Dennis, when not in a factory entry, Niki won 3 races for P4 plus the series. Decades later he won a BMW Procar exhibition race event before the German Grand Prix of 2008.

Lauda finished 4th in Monza in September then won the non-WC Imola event, still with the Alfa V12 engine, before Brabham returned to the familiar Cosworth V8. During practice for the 1979 Canadian Grand Prix later that month, Niki told Ecclestone that he wanted to retire, as he had no more desire to "drive around in circles". Having founded Lauda Air, a charter airline, he returned to Austria to run the company full-time.

Niki returned to racing during 1982, for an unprecedented $3 million salary, when following a successful test with McLaren, he had to convince team sponsor Marlboro that he was still capable of winning. Lauda did so in his third race back, winning the Long Beach Grand Prix. Before the opening race of the season at Kyalami race track in South Africa, he was the organiser of the so-called "drivers' strike", Niki having seen that the new Super Licence required the drivers to commit themselves to their present teams, realising that it could damage a driver's negotiating position. The drivers, with the exception of Teo Fabi, barricaded themselves into a banqueting suite at Sunnyside Park Hotel until their demands were met.

The following season was transitional for the McLaren team, as they made a change from Ford-Cosworth power to TAG-badged Porsche turbo power, Lauda failing to win a race in 1983, his highest finish being 2nd at Long Beach, behind his teammate John Watson. Some political maneuvering by Niki forced a furious chief designer John Barnard to design an interim car earlier than planned to get the TAG-Porsche engine some much needed race testing, Lauda nearly winning the final race of the season in South Africa.

Niki won a third world championship during 1984 by half a point, ahead of teammate Alain Prost, due to only half points being awarded for that season's shortened Monaco Grand Prix. His Austrian Grand Prix victory that year was the only time an Austrian has won his home Grand Prix. At first, Lauda didn't want Alain to become his teammate, as he was a much faster rival but during their two seasons together, they had a good relationship, Niki later saying that beating the talented Frenchman was a big motivator for him.

The whole season was dominated by Lauda and Prost, who won 12 of 16 races between them, Niki winning 5 races, while Alain won 7. However, Lauda, who'd set a record for the most pole positions in a season during 1975, rarely matched his teammate in qualifying, despite which, Niki's championship win came in Portugal, when he had to start in 11th place on the grid, while Prost qualified on the front row.

Alain did everything he could, starting from 2nd to win his 7th race of the season, but Lauda's calculating drive, including setting the fastest race lap, passing car after car, led to him finishing just behind his teammate, giving him enough points to lift his third title. His runner up position was fortunate though, as Nigel Mansell was in 2nd for much of the race.

However, as it was Nigel's last race with Lotus before joining Williams in 1985, Lotus boss Peter Warr refused to give Mansell the brakes he wanted for his car, so the Englishman retired with brake failure on lap 52. As Niki had passed the Toleman of F1 rookie Ayrton Senna for third place only a few laps earlier, Nigel's retirement took him to 2nd behind Prost.

The following season was a disappointment for Lauda, with 11 retirements from the 14 races he started. He didn't start the Belgian Grand Prix at Spa-Francorchamps after crashing then breaking his wrist during practice, later missing the European Grand Prix at Brands Hatch, with John Watson replacing him for that race.

Niki did manage 4th at the San Marino Grand Prix, 5th at the German Grand Prix, and a single race win at the Dutch Grand Prix, where he held off a fast finishing Prost late in the race. It was his last Grand Prix victory and the last Formula One Grand Prix held in the Netherlands. After announcing his retirement at the Austrian Grand Prix of 1985, he retired for good at the end of that season.

Lauda's final Formula One Grand Prix drive was the inaugural Australian Grand Prix in Adelaide, South Australia, when after qualifying 16th, a steady drive took him into the lead by lap 53. However, his McLaren's ceramic brakes suffered on the street circuit, so he crashed out of the lead at the end of the long Brabham Straight on lap 57 when his brakes finally failed. Niki was one of only two drivers in the race who'd driven in the non-championship Australian Grand Prix of 1984, the other being

1982 World Champion Keke Rosberg, who won in Adelaide during 1985, before replacing Lauda at McLaren the following season.

Niki's Ferrari helmet was originally a plain red with his full name written on both sides and the Raiffeisen Bank logo in the chin area. He wore a modified AGV helmet in the weeks following his Nürburgring accident, so the lining wouldn't aggravate his burned scalp too badly. Upon his return to McLaren in 1982, his helmet was white, having featured the red "L" logo of Lauda Air instead of his name on both sides, complete with branding from his personal sponsor Parmalat on the top. From 1983–1985, the red and white were reversed to evoke memories of his earlier helmet design.

Niki returned to Formula One in a managerial position during 1993, when Luca di Montezemolo offered him a consulting role at Ferrari. Halfway through the season of 2001 Lauda became team principal of the Jaguar Formula One team, which failed to improve so Niki was made redundant, together with 70 other key figures, at the end of 2002. Lauda was appointed non-executive chairman of the Mercedes AMG Petronas F1 Team in September 2012, having taken part in the negotiations to sign Lewis Hamilton to a 3-year deal with AMG Mercedes.

Niki went back to running his airline, Lauda Air, following his 2nd Formula One retirement in 1985, having been appointed consultant at Ferrari as part of an effort by Montezemolo to rejuvenate the team during his time as airline manager. After selling his Lauda Air shares to majority partner Austrian Airlines in 1999, he managed the Jaguar Formula One racing team from 2001 to 2002.

He started a new airline, Niki, during late 2003, which in similar fashion to Lauda Air, was merged with its major partner Air Berlin in 2011. Niki took over chartered airline Amira Air during early 2016, renaming the company LaudaMotion. Due to Air Berlin's insolvency the following year, LaudaMotion took over the Niki brand and asset after an unsuccessful bid by Lufthansa and IAG. Lauda held a commercial pilot's licence, having acted as a captain on the flights of his airline from time to time.

Niki was inducted into the International Motorsports Hall of Fame in 1993 then from 1996 provided commentary on Grands Prix for Austrian and German TV on RTL. He was criticized for calling Robert Kubica a "polacke", an ethnic slur for Polish people, on air during May 2010 at the Monaco Grand Prix.

Lauda has sometimes been known by the nickname "the rat", "SuperRat" or "King Rat," because of his prominent buck teeth. He was associated with both Parmalat and Viessmann, sponsoring the cap he wore from 1976 to hide the severe burns he sustained in his Nurburgring accident. Niki stated in a 2009 interview with the German newspaper Die Zeit that an advertiser was paying €1.2m for the space on his red cap.

The Austrian post office issued a stamp honouring Lauda during 2005, before American sports TV network ESPN ranked him 22nd of their top drivers of all-time. Niki wrote 5 books: The Art and Science of Grand Prix Driving, which was titled Formula 1:

The Art and Technicalities of Grand Prix Driving in some countries (1975); My Years With Ferrari (1978); The New Formula One: A Turbo Age (1984); Meine Story, titled To Hell and Back in some markets (1986); Das dritte Leben (en. The third life)(1996). Lauda credited Austrian journalist Herbert Volker with editing the books.

Film and television

The F1 battle between Niki Lauda and James Hunt of 1976 was dramatized in the movie, Rush (2013), where Niki was played by Daniel Brühl, Lauda having made a cameo appearance at the end of the film. Niki said of Hunt's death, "When I heard he'd died aged 45 of a heart attack I wasn't surprised, I was just sad." Lauda also said that James was one of the very few he liked, a smaller number of people he respected and the only person he'd envied. Niki appeared in an episode of Mayday titled "Niki Lauda: Testing the Limits," covering the events of Lauda Air Flight 004.

Niki's first wife was Marlene Knaus, whom he wed in 1976 then divorced during 1991, the couple had two sons Mathias, who became a racing driver, and Lukas, who was Mathias's manager. Lauda married Birgit Wetzinger in 2008, a flight attendant at his airline, who'd donated a kidney to Niki in 2005, when the kidney he received from his brother during 1997 failed. Birgit gave birth to twins during September 2009. It was announced on 2nd August 2018 that Lauda had successfully undergone a lung transplant operation in his native Austria.

Niki died in his sleep on 20th May 2019, aged 70, at the University Hospital of Zürich, where he had been undergoing dialysis treatment for kidney problems, following a period of ill health. A statement issued on behalf of his family reported that he'd died peacefully, surrounded by them.

Racing record

Complete European Formula Two Championship results

(key) (Races in bold indicate pole position; races in italics indicate fastest lap)

Year	Entrant	Chassis	Engine
Pos.	Pts		

1	2	3	4	5	6	7	8
9	10	11	12	13	14		

1971	March Engineering		March 712M		Cosworth FVA		
HOC							

Ret	THR	10	NÜR	6	JAR	7 PAL	DNQ
	ROU	4 MAN	Ret	TUL	Ret	ALB	Ret
	VAL	7 VAL	10th	8			

1972	March Engineering		March 722		Ford BDA		

MAL	2 THR	3 HOC	Ret	PAU	Ret	PAL	DNQ
	HOC	Ret	ROU	Ret	ÖST	Ret	IMO 3
	MAN	Ret	PER	SAL 6	ALB	HOC 9	5th
25							

Complete Formula One World Championship results

Year   Entrant Chassis Engine

1	2	3	4	5	6	7	8
9	10	11	12	13	14	15	
16	17	WDC	Pts				

1971   STP March Racing Team March 711   Ford Cosworth DFV 3.0 V8

RSA	ESP	MON	NED	FRA	GBR	GER	AUT	Ret
	ITA	CAN	USA	NC	0			

1972   STP March Racing Team March 721   Ford Cosworth DFV 3.0 V8

ARG	11	RSA	7 NC	0

March 721X

ESP	Ret	MON	16	BEL	12

March 721G

FRA	Ret	GBR	9	GER	Ret	AUT	10	ITA	13
CAN	DSQ	USA	NC						

1973   Marlboro-BRM BRM P160C   BRM P142 3.0 V12

ARG	Ret	BRA	8

BRM P160D

RSA   Ret

BRM P160E

ESP Ret   BEL 5   MON Ret SWE 13   FRA 9 GBR
12   NED Ret   GER Ret   AUT DNS   ITA
Ret   CAN Ret   USA Ret

18th   2

1974   Scuderia Ferrari SpA SEFAC   Ferrari 312B3
Ferrari 001/11 3.0 F12

ARG 2 BRA Ret   RSA 16   ESP 1   BEL 2
       MON Ret   SWE Ret   NED 1   FRA 2
       GBR 5 GER Ret   AUT Ret   ITA Ret CAN
Ret   USA Ret   4th   38

1975   Scuderia Ferrari SpA SEFAC   Ferrari 312B3
Ferrari 001/11 3.0 F12

ARG 6 BRA 5

Ferrari 312T   Ferrari 015 3.0 F12

RSA 5 ESP Ret   MON 1 BEL 1 SWE 1 NED 2 FRA 1
       GBR 8 GER 3 AUT 6 ITA 3 USA 1   1st
       64.5

1976   Scuderia Ferrari SpA SEFAC   Ferrari 312T   Ferrari
015 3.0 F12

BRA 1 RSA 1 USW 2

Ferrari 312T2

ESP 2 BEL 1   MON 1   SWE 3 FRA Ret   GBR 1
GER Ret   AUT   NED   ITA 4 CAN 8 USA 3 JPN
Ret   2nd   68

1977   Scuderia Ferrari SpA SEFAC   Ferrari 312T2
Ferrari 015 3.0 F12

ARG Ret BRA 3 RSA 1   USW 2 ESP DNS MON 2
BEL 2 SWE Ret FRA 5   GBR 2 GER 1   AUT 2
NED 1 ITA 2   USA 4   CAN   JPN   1st   72

1978   Parmalat Racing Team   Brabham BT45CAlfa Romeo
115-12 3.0 F12

ARG 2 BRA 3

Brabham BT46

RSA Ret   USW Ret   MON 2   BEL Ret
        ESP Ret   FRA Ret   GBR 2 GER Ret
        AUT Ret   NED 3 ITA 1 USA Ret   CAN
Ret

Brabham BT46B

SWE   1   4th   44

1979   Parmalat Racing Team   Brabham BT48 Alfa Romeo
1260 3.0 V12

ARG   Ret   BRA   Ret RSA 6   USW   Ret ESP Ret BEL
Ret   MON Ret FRA Ret   GBR Ret   GER Ret
         AUT Ret   NED Ret   ITA   4

Brabham BT49 Ford Cosworth DFV 3.0 V8
                                 CAN   WD   USA   4
         14th

1982   Marlboro McLaren International   McLaren MP4B
         Ford Cosworth DFV 3.0 V8   RSA   4   BRA   Ret
         USW   1SMR   BEL   DSQ   MON   Ret   DET
Ret   CAN   Ret NED   4   GBR   1   FRA   8   GER   DNS
         AUT   5   SUI   3   ITA   Ret   CPL   Ret
         5th   30

1983   Marlboro McLaren International   McLaren
MP4/1C   Ford Cosworth DFV 3.0 V8   BRA   3 USW
2

Ford Cosworth DFY 3.0 V8

FRA Ret   SMR Ret   MON DNQ   BEL Ret
     DET Ret   CAN Ret   GBR 6 GER DSQ
     AUT 6

McLaren MP4/1E   TAG TTE PO1 1.5 V6t
                                        NED Ret   ITA
Ret   EUR Ret   RSA 11   10th   12

1984   Marlboro McLaren International   McLaren MP4/2
        TAG TTE PO1 1.5 V6t   BRA

Ret   RSA 1 BEL Ret   SMR Ret   FRA 1 MON
Ret   CAN 2 DET Ret   DAL Ret   GBR 1 GER 2
       AUT 1 NED 2 ITA 1 EUR 4 POR 2   1st
       72

1985   Marlboro McLaren International   McLaren
MP4/2B   TAG TTE PO1 1.5 V6t

BRA Ret   POR Ret SMR 4 MON Ret CAN Ret DET
Ret   FRA Ret GBR Ret   GER 5 AUT Ret   NED 1
ITA Ret   BEL DNS   EUR   RSA Ret AUS Ret
       10th   14

Complete Formula One Non-Championship results

Year   Entrant Chassis Engine 1   2   3   4
       5   6

1972   STP March Racing Team March 721   Ford Cosworth DFV 3.0 V8

ROC   BRA   INT   OUL   REP DNS   VIC

1973   Marlboro-BRM BRM P160D   BRM P142 3.0 V12

ROC Ret   INT 5

1974   Scuderia Ferrari SpA SEFAC   Ferrari 312B3   Ferrari 001/11 3.0 F12

PRE   ROC 2 INT

1975   Scuderia Ferrari SpA SEFAC   Ferrari 312T   Ferrari 015 3.0 F12

ROC   INT 1 SUI

1976   Scuderia Ferrari SpA SEFAC   Ferrari 312T2   Ferrari 015 3.0 F12

ROC Ret   INT

1978   Parmalat Racing Team   Brabham BT45CAlfa Romeo 115-12 3.0 F12

INT DNS

1979   Parmalat Racing Team   Brabham BT48 Alfa Romeo 1260 3.0 V12

ROC 5 GNM   DIN 1

Books

Lauda, Niki. Technik und Praxis des Grand-Prix-Sports (in German). Stuttgart; Vienna: Stuttgart Motorbuch-Verlag; Orac.

——. The Art and Science of Grand Prix Driving (AKA Formula 1: The Art and Technicalities of Grand Prix Driving). David Irving (trans.). Osceola, Wis.: Motorbooks International. ISBN 9780879380496. OCLC 483675371.

—— (1977). Protokoll: meine Jahre mit Ferrari. Stuttgart; Vienna: Stuttgart Motorbuch-Verlag; Orac. ISBN 9783853688434. OCLC 3869352.

—— (1978). My Years with Ferrari. Osceola, Wis.: Motorbooks International. ISBN 9780879380595. OCLC 3842607. AKA For the Record: My Years with Ferrari (British edition).

—— (1982). Die neue Formel 1. Stuttgart; Vienna: Stuttgart Motorbuch-Verlag; Orac. ISBN 9783853689103. OCLC 1072406853.

—— (1984). The New Formula One: A Turbo Age. Osceola, Wis.: Motorbooks International. ISBN 9780879381790. OCLC 10456956.

——; Völker, Herbert (1985). Niki Lauda: Meine Story. Stuttgart; Vienna: Stuttgart Motorbuch-Verlag; Orac. ISBN 9783701500253. OCLC 38110109.

——; Völker, Herbert (1986). To Hell and Back: An Autobiography. E. J. Crockett (trans.). London: Stanley Paul. ISBN 9780091642402. OCLC 476752274.

——. Das dritte Leben. Munich: Heyne. ISBN 9783453115729. OCLC 40286522.

Awards and achievements

Preceded by Franz Klammer

Austrian Sportsman of the year

1977

Succeeded by Sepp Walcher

Preceded by Nadia Comăneci

BBC Overseas Sports Personality of the Year 1977

Succeeded by Muhammad Ali

Preceded by Nelson Piquet

Autosport International Racing Driver Award 1984

Succeeded by Alain Prost

Sporting positions

Preceded by James Hunt

BRDC International Trophy winner 1975

Succeeded by

James Hunt

Preceded by

Emerson Fittipaldi

Formula One World Champion 1975

Succeeded by James Hunt

Preceded by

James Hunt

Formula One World Champion 1977

Succeeded by Mario Andretti

Preceded by None

Procar BMW M1 Champion 1979

Succeeded by Nelson Piquet

Preceded by Nelson Piquet

Formula One World Champion 1984

Succeeded by Alain Prost

It must've been disconcerting for passengers to learn that their pilot was best known for his spectacular crashes but travellers on Niki Lauda's low-cost airline, Niki, had to get used to the formula one champion's clipped Austrian tones from the cockpit. A commercial pilot with 13,000 hours of flying under his belt, Lauda took personal command of one of the airline's 5 Airbus jets at least twice / week, insisting that his speed freak days were behind him: "Racing is the opposite of flying. In racing, you want to win - there are no rules and you can do whatever you want. Flying a plane is the opposite: you respect rules and fly to the rules. You can't possibly compare the two."

Niki's life gave new meaning to the tag "survivor". When he was dragged from the burning wreckage of his Ferrari at the German grand prix of 1976, his injuries were so severe that a priest gave him the last rites but he astonished fans by returning to racing just 30 days later then went on to win 2 more world titles. With a mangled right ear and a face puckered with scar tissue, Lauda's appearance was an eternal reminder of his experience in battle, a red baseball cap hiding the worst of the fire damage to his scalp.

Since his retirement from sport, Lauda's business career had been just as volcanic, having quit the board of Lauda Air, his first aviation venture, amid boardroom acrimony, with losses of over $60m. A return to the racetrack as boss of the Jaguar team lasted for just one dismal season before he was sacked in 2002 but Niki was on the comeback trail again. Sitting under an elaborate oil painting of a stern 18th-century Frau at the Austrian embassy, he introduced British travellers to his new concept - a budget airline that served free food and drinks, which he hoped would be Austria's answer to easyJet and Ryanair.

Niki began a route between Stansted and Vienna, flying in the cockpit, the airline serving half-a-dozen other cities from its Vienna hub, having a partnership deal with Germany's Air Berlin. It had struck an ambitious deal with Airbus to triple the size of its 5-strong fleet, with deliveries to begin the following year: "I like the mode of business of aviation. It's a risky business with difficulties which you can fill with innovative ideas and different things."

Challenges had been plentiful since he'd set up the airline that November. Fuel prices had rocketed by 80% since the following March, with rivals having predicted a "bloodbath" among smaller operators. "September 11 gave a big downdraft to all airlines," Lauda conceded. "When you start at the worst time, you have to find a structure with which you can survive."

Niki brushed aside the gloomy predictions of bankruptcies made by Ryanair's boss, Michael O'Leary: "There's always this typical talk of big airlines. We'll survive if we do a better job. All you need is a lower cost structure and to find enough passengers to pay for it." Lauda dismissed the threat of the "cattle airlines", stressing that although its fares began at £19.95, Niki was a class above the rest. Its cabin crew were clad in shiny silver Star Trek chic, Lauda saying its sandwiches were made by one of Austria's top caterers.

Niki's focus on driving down costs extended to a refusal to recognise unions, having been scathing about Austria's aviation union, saying its efforts were targeted at making other airlines as expensive as the country's two main carriers - Tyrolean and Austrian Airlines. "I've never signed a union contract. I'd rather keep them out, purely and simply."

The dislike was mutual, the Austrian Cockpit Association having questioned the pay and contract structure on which Niki's crew were employed. The union's vice-president, Siegfried Lenz, described Lauda as "a very tough and ruthless businessman. His success as a businessman has been mostly for himself and not for the businesses he's operated."

Brisk and businesslike in person, Niki had a reputation for demanding exacting standards. Born during 1949 into a family of Viennese industrialists, he completed his apprenticeship as a motor mechanic before becoming swept up in racing when aged 18. After winning his formula one titles in 1975 and 1977, he founded Lauda Air, with two Fokker aircraft.

It struggled during the early '80s but eventually established itself with a 25-strong fleet, providing long-haul flights around the globe. Niki suffered a shattering blow when a Lauda Air Boeing 767 crashed in Thailand in 1991, killing all 223 passengers. He flew to the jungle to search for clues about the electrical failure that caused the tragedy, the airline being cleared of all blame.

Problems mounted when Lauda's strategic partner, Lufthansa, sold a 36% stake to Austrian Airlines, prompting a series of rows which sent the carrier spiralling into the red. "The avalanche of Austrian came down on Lauda and smashed it. I realised the cultural differences weren't acceptable to me." Niki quit the board, but not before a report by accountants KPMG had criticised his tenure, citing poor financial controls over foreign currencies within the business.

Hurt by the criticism, Lauda left Vienna for London to join Ford's Jaguar racing team, being reported as saying he was through with Austria, having been "brutally driven out like a dog". He'd since moved back, stating that he'd said no such thing. Outside of the aviation business, Niki had established a unique car hire firm, Lauda Motion, which rented out Smart cars for €1 / day in Vienna and Munich, making its money by selling advertising space on the bodywork of its 150-strong fleet.

Niki traveled to every grand prix to commentate for German TV - so what did he think of the state of his old sport, under the dominance of Michael Schumacher? "You have to bear in mind that what Ferrari and Schumacher did this year was unique. They did a perfect job," said Lauda. To the casual observer, he agreed that this made poor viewing: "For people who don't know how much work goes into such a success, I believe it is boring."

Niki argued that Ferrari's success in virtually eradicating technical faults was astonishing, adding: "Next year, in the new year, we've got new rules. You can only hope that some of the British cars get competitive and that we're going to have better racing." Lauda had little sympathy for the British Racing Drivers' Club's protests against the demise of that year's Silverstone grand prix, which he said offered embarrassingly poor transport facilities for spectators. "It's up to the organisers to make it happen. There are so many other grands prix around the world happening, why the British fail to get things right I do not understand."

Niki's youngest son, Matthias, was a formula 3000 driver, having overridden the objections of his parents. Lauda's assessment of his offspring's talent was unsentimental: "He has speed, there's no question but he makes a lot of mistakes. He's got a lot to learn." Experience had taught Lauda the virtue of caution, his new airline being set to expand - but only gradually. The 5-strong fleet would double in size by 2011, Niki saying: "I'm going to grow it in a conservative way. We wait until one route makes money before we launch another."

Air Berlin, a better established low-cost carrier from Germany, which had bought a 24% stake in Niki was providing back-up through its bookings system and administration. Niki's load factors were running at 81%, Lauda expecting 960,000 passengers to travel on the carrier that year, producing £48m of turnover, which he said would produce a profit.

Despite naming the airline after himself, Niki insisted that he disliked notoriety: "I hate being famous. You have no freedom. You can't do anything." One of the most famous living Austrians, he was a folk hero at home, his departure from Lauda Air having prompted a rash of "Niki Come Back" T-shirts, with expressions of outrage coming from the country's deputy chancellor downwards.

In its lower echelons, Lauda said fame had its perks: "You get your passport quicker, you can argue with a friendly policeman not to pay a fine but if you're known in too many places, it's difficult, because you always have to behave well, you're always watched and you just can't do anything." Lauda Air was still flying, as the leisure flights arm of Austrian Airlines, with an indefinite licence to use his name, Niki conceding: "I was the idiot who signed away the name." If it all went wrong for him a

2nd time, there was a back-up plan. His full name was Andreas Nikolas Lauda. "Andreas could be the name for my third airline. Unfortunately nobody's ever heard of it."

The sport of Formula One united to pay tribute to the courage and bravery of its 3-times world champion, Niki Lauda, who'd died aged 70. The Austrian died in Vienna 9 months after receiving a lung transplant. Lauda, who won titles in 1975, 1977 and 1984, was hugely admired, respected and liked within F1 after a remarkable career, during which he won two titles for Ferrari and one for McLaren, having come back from an horrific accident in 1976.

Trapped in his burning car at the German Grand Prix, he was pulled from the wreckage, but not before suffering severe burns and damage to his lungs. Overcoming doubts that he'd ever race again, Niki's determination to do so was extraordinary as just 6 weeks later he returned for the Italian Grand Prix, still bandaged and in pain after extensive surgery.

Sir Jackie Stewart, 79, a fellow 3-times world champion who raced alongside Lauda during the early '70s, said. "Niki had a degree of bravery that I'd never seen the like of before. I remember seeing Niki put his helmet on, and his wounds were still absolutely obvious. To be brave enough to put on the helmet was amazing, but then he went out and qualified 5th. He will not go down as just one of the best drivers of all time, but one of the most courageous, too. Niki Lauda will be remembered forever."

Lauda competed in 171 races, winning 25. He also had business interests including his own airlines, having gone on to have senior roles in F1 management, most recently as non-executive chairman of the hugely successful Mercedes team since 2012, to which he helped sign the British world champion Lewis Hamilton, who paid an emotional tribute to Niki on Instagram:

"My buddy, I'm struggling to believe you're gone. I'll miss our conversations, our laughs, the big hugs after winning races together. It's truly been an honour working alongside you over these past 7 years. I wouldn't even have been in this team if it wasn't for you. God rest your soul. Thank you for being a bright light in my life. I'll always be here for your family should they ever need me. Love you man. Your friend always, Lewis."

Toto Wolff, the team principal at Mercedes, said: "Niki will always remain one of the greatest legends of our sport – he combined heroism, humanity and honesty inside and outside the cockpit. His passing leaves a void in Formula One. We haven't just lost a hero who staged the most remarkable comeback ever seen, but also a man who brought precious clarity and candour. Our Mercedes team has also lost a guiding light. Niki, you're quite simply irreplaceable, there will never be another like you. It was our honour to call you our chairman – and my privilege to call you my friend."

"Everyone who was in Formula One knew Niki's personality as one of the most potent individuals in the sport," Damon Hill told Sky Sports. He was highly intellectual, stoic, someone who didn't have time for any of the BS in the business at all. He was eminently quotable all the time. It's very sad to hear that we've lost Niki, but so many people have been affected positively by having known him."

Chase Carey, chairman and chief executive of the Formula One group, issued a statement: "Formula 1 has lost not only one of the truly great exponents of the sport but also one of its heroes. His love of racing and the courage he demonstrated were simply extraordinary and he inspired so many fans. His passing is a great loss for the entire Formula 1 family and motorsport as a whole. All our thoughts go out to his family."

Nico Rosberg, F1's world champion of 2016 with Mercedes, tweeted: "Dear Niki. Thank you for everything that you did for me. I learned so much from you. Your passion, your fighting spirit ... myself and all of your fans around the world are thinking of you and your family and wish that you Rest in Peace." A number of tributes to Lauda were expected to take place at the following weekend's Monaco Grand Prix.

33

Michael Schumacher, born on 3rd January 1969, Hürth, North Rhine-Westphalia, West Germany, is a retired racing driver who raced in Formula One for Jordan Grand Prix, Benetton and Ferrari, where he spent most of his career, followed by Mercedes upon his return to the sport. Widely regarded as one of the greatest Formula One drivers ever, Schumacher is the only driver in history to win 7 Formula One World Championships, 5 of which he won successively. Michael also holds the records for the most Grand Prix wins (91), the most fastest laps (77) and the most races won in a single season (13), being "statistically the greatest driver the sport has ever seen" at the time of his retirement from the sport, as stated on the official Formula One website, .

Following his success in karting as a child, Schumacher won titles in Formula König and Formula Three, before joining Mercedes in the World Sportscar Championship. Michael's Mercedes-funded race debut for the Jordan Formula One team during 1991 led to him being signed by Benetton for the rest of that season. He finished third the following year then 4th in the next, before becoming the first German World Drivers' Champion during 1994, just a point ahead of Damon Hill, in controversial circumstances.

Schumacher successfully defended his title the following season, with a greater margin of victory. He then moved to Ferrari, which had last won the Drivers' Championship in 1979, helping transform them into the most successful team in Formula One history, as he came close to winning the 1997 & 1998 titles, before breaking his leg at the British Grand Prix of 1999, ending another title run.

Michael won 5 successive World Drivers' Championships from 2000 - 2004, including an unprecedented 6th and 7th title, lifting the trophy with a record 6 races remaining during 2002, finishing on the podium in every race. Schumacher won 12 out of the first 13 races in 2004, going on to triumph a record 13 times as he won his final title. Michael retired from Formula One during 2006, after finishing runner-up to Renault's Fernando Alonso, before returning to Formula One in 2010 with Mercedes. He had the fastest qualifying time at the Monaco Grand Prix of 2012, reaching his only podium on his return at that year's European Grand Prix, where he finished third. Schumacher announced that October he'd be retiring for a 2nd time at the end of the season.

Michael's career was often controversial, having twice been involved in collisions during the final race of a season that determined the outcome of the World Championship, with Damon Hill in 1994 in Adelaide then with Jacques Villeneuve during 1997 in Jerez. Schumacher became an ambassador for UNESCO, having been involved in many humanitarian efforts during his life, donating tens of millions of dollars to charity.

Michael and his younger brother, Ralf Schumacher, are the only siblings to have won races in Formula One, having been the first brothers to finish 1st and 2nd in the same race, a feat they repeated in 4 races. Michael suffered a traumatic brain injury in a skiing accident on 29th December 2013, being placed in a medically induced coma for 6 months until 16th June 2014, when he left the hospital in Grenoble for further rehabilitation at the University Hospital of Lausanne. Schumacher was moved to his home on 9th September that year where he has continued to receive medical treatment and rehabilitation. Michael remained unable to walk or stand by 2016, former

Ferrari manager, Jean Todt having said in July 2019 that Schumacher was making "good progress" but "struggles to communicate".

Michael is the son of Rolf Schumacher, a bricklayer, and his wife Elisabeth. When Michael was aged 4, his father modified his pedal kart by adding a small motorcycle engine. When he crashed it into a lamp post in Kerpen, his parents took him to the karting track at Kerpen-Horrem, where Schumacher became the youngest member of the karting club. His father soon built him a kart from discarded parts then at the age of 6 he won his first club championship.

To support his son's racing, Rolf took on a 2nd job renting and repairing karts, while his wife worked at the track's canteen, but when Michael needed a new engine costing 800 DM, his parents weren't able to afford it, although he continued racing with the support of local businessmen. Regulations in Germany require a driver to be at least 14 years old to get a kart license, so Schumacher got one in Luxembourg when aged 12.

Michael obtained his German license during 1983, a year after he won the German Junior Kart Championship then won many German and European kart championships from the next year onwards. Schumacher joined Eurokart dealer Adolf Neubert in 1985 becoming the German and European kart champion by 1987 then left school to begin working as a mechanic. The following year he made his first step into single-seat car racing by taking part in the German Formula Ford and Formula König series, winning the latter.

Michael signed with Willi Weber's WTS Formula Three team during 1989, Willi funding him as he competed in the German Formula 3 series, lifting the title the following year, while also winning the Macau Grand Prix. Along with his Formula 3 rivals Heinz-Harald Frentzen and Karl Wendlinger, Schumacher joined the Mercedes junior racing programme in the World Sports-Prototype Championship towards the end of 1990.

This was unusual for a young driver, with most of Michael's contemporaries competing in Formula 3000 on the way to Formula One but Weber advised Schumacher that being exposed to professional press conferences and driving powerful cars in long distance races would help his career. In the World Sportscar Championship season of 1990, Michael won the season finale at the Autódromo Hermanos Rodríguez in a Sauber–Mercedes C11, finishing 5th in the drivers' championship despite only driving in 3 of the 9 races.

Schumacher continued with the team in the World Sportscar Championship season of 1991, again winning the final race of the season at Autopolis in Japan with a Sauber–Mercedes-Benz C291, leading to a 9th-place finish in the drivers' championship. Michael also competed at Le Mans during that season, finishing 5th in a car shared with Karl Wendlinger and Fritz Kreutzpointner, having driven in one race in the Japanese Formula 3000 Championship, finishing 2nd.

Schumacher was known throughout his career for his ability to produce fast laps at crucial moments in a race and to push his car to the very limit for sustained periods. Motor sport author Christopher Hilton wrote in 2003 that a "measure of a driver's capabilities is his performance in wet races, because the most delicate car control and sensitivity are needed". Hilton observed that like other great drivers, Michael's record in wet conditions indicated very few mistakes, having won 17 of the 30 races that he'd contested in the wet up to the end of that season.

Some of Schumacher's best performances occurred in such conditions, earning him the nicknames "Regenkönig" (rain king) or "Regenmeister" (rain master), even in the non-German-language media. He became known as "the Red Baron", because of his red Ferrari, in reference to the German Manfred von Richthofen, the famous flying ace of World War I, Michael's other nicknames having included "Schumi", "Schuey" and "Schu".

Schumacher is often credited with having popularized Formula One in Germany, where it was formerly regarded as a fringe sport. When Michael first retired during 2006, of the top 10 drivers 3 were German, more than any other nationality and more than ever before in Formula One history. Younger German drivers, including Sebastian Vettel, felt that Schumacher had been key to their having become Formula One drivers. Michael was the president of the Grand Prix Drivers' Association for the latter part of his Formula One career, being voted the most popular driver of the season among Formula One fans in a FIA survey during 2006.

Schumacher made his Formula One debut with the Jordan-Ford team at the Belgian Grand Prix of 1991, driving car # 32 as a replacement for the imprisoned Bertrand Gachot. Michael, still a contracted Mercedes driver, was signed by Eddie Jordan after Mercedes paid Jordan $150,000 for his debut. The week before the race, he impressed Jordan designer Gary Anderson and team manager Trevor Foster during a test drive at Silverstone.

His manager Willi Weber assured Jordan that Schumacher knew the challenging Spa track well, although he'd really only seen it as a spectator. During the race weekend, teammate Andrea de Cesaris was meant to show Michael the circuit, but was held up with contract negotiations, so he learned the track on his own, by cycling around it on a fold-up bike he'd brought with him.

Schumacher impressed the paddock by qualifying 7th in the race, matching the team's season-best grid position, out-qualifying 11-year veteran de Cesaris. Motorsport journalist Joe Saward stated that after qualifying "clumps of German journalists were talking about 'the best talent since Stefan Bellof'" but Michael retired on the first lap of the race with clutch problems.

Following his Belgian Grand Prix debut, despite an agreement in principle between Jordan and Schumacher's Mercedes management that the German would race for the Irish team for the rest of the season, Michael was engaged by Benetton-Ford for the following race. Jordan applied for an injunction in the UK courts to stop him driving for Benetton, but lost the case because they hadn't signed a final contract. Schumacher finished the season of 1991 with 4 points from 6 races, his best finish being 5th in his 2nd race, the Italian Grand Prix, in which he finished ahead of his teammate, 3-time World Champion Nelson Piquet.

At the start of the following season, the Sauber team, planning their Formula One debut with Mercedes backing for 1993, invoked a clause in Michael's contract that stated that if Mercedes entered Formula One, he'd drive for them. However, it was agreed that Schumacher would stay with Benetton, Peter

Sauber saying that he "didn't want to drive for us. Why would I have forced him?".

The season of 1992 was dominated by the Williams of Nigel Mansell and Riccardo Patrese, featuring powerful Renault engines, semi-automatic gearboxes and active suspension to control the car's ride height. In the 'conventional' Benetton B192 Michael took a place on the podium for the first time, finishing third in the Mexican Grand Prix. He went on to drive to his first victory at the Belgian Grand Prix, in a wet race at the Spa-Francorchamps circuit, which he said in 2003 was "far and away my favourite track". Schumacher finished third in the Drivers' Championship of 1992 with 53 points, 3 points behind runner-up Patrese.

The Williams of Damon Hill and Alain Prost dominated the following season, Benetton introducing their own active suspension and traction control early that year, last of the frontrunning teams to do so. Michael won one race, the Portuguese Grand Prix, where he beat Prost, having had 9 podium finishes, but retired in 7 of the other 15 races. He finished the season in 4th, with 52 points.

Schumacher drove the Benetton B194 to his first World Championship in 1994 but the season was marred by the death of Ayrton Senna, which he witnessed, having been directly behind in 2nd position, Roland Ratzenberger also having died during the San Marino Grand Prix. There were also allegations that several teams, particularly Michael's Benetton team, broke the sport's technical regulations.

Schumacher won 6 of the first 7 races, having led the Spanish Grand Prix, before a gearbox failure left him stuck in 5th gear, so he finished the race in 2nd place. After the San Marino Grand

Prix, the Benetton, Ferrari and McLaren teams were investigated following suspicions that they'd broken the FIA-imposed ban on electronic aids. Benetton and McLaren initially refused to hand over their source code for investigation but when they did so, the FIA discovered hidden functionality in both teams' software, but no evidence that it had been used in a race.

Both teams were fined $100,000 for their initial refusal to cooperate, but the McLaren software, which was a gearbox program that allowed automatic shifts, was deemed legal. The Benetton software was deemed to be a form of "launch control" that would've allowed Michael to make perfect starts, which was explicitly outlawed by the regulations. However, there was no evidence to suggest that the software had been used.

Schumacher was penalised for overtaking on the formation lap at the British Grand Prix. He then ignored the penalty and the subsequent black flag, which indicates that the driver must return to the pits, for which he was disqualified, later being given a two-race ban, Benetton blaming the incident on a communication error between the stewards and the team.

Michael was also disqualified after winning the Belgian Grand Prix when his car was found to have illegal wear on its skidblock, a measure used after the accidents at Imola to limit downforce, thus cornering speed. Benetton protested that the skidblock had been damaged when Schumacher spun over a kerb, but the FIA rejected their appeal because of the pattern of wear and damage visible on the block.

These incidents helped Damon Hill to close the points gap, so Michael led by just one point going into the final race in Australia. He hit the guardrail on the outside of the track while leading on lap 36, with Hill trying to pass, but as Schumacher's car returned to the track there was a collision on the corner resulting in them both having to retire. Michael thus won a very controversial championship, the first German to do so, Jochen Rindt having raced under the Austrian flag. At the FIA conference after the race, the new World Champion dedicated his title to Ayrton Senna.

Schumacher comfortably defended his title with Benetton during 1995, having had the same Renault engine as Williams, with 33 more points than 2nd-placed Damon Hill. With teammate Johnny Herbert, he took Benetton to its first Constructors' Championship, becoming the youngest two-time World Champion in Formula One history. The season was marred by several collisions with Damon, an overtaking manoeuvre by Hill having taken them both out of the British Grand Prix on lap 45 then again on lap 23 of the Italian Grand Prix. Michael won 9 of the 17 races, having finished on the podium 11 times, only once qualifying lower than 4th, at the Belgian Grand Prix, in 16th, but still went on to win the race.

Schumacher then joined Ferrari, a team that had last won the Drivers' Championship in 1979 and the Constructors' Championship during 1983, for a salary of $60 million over 2 years. He left Benetton a year before his contract with them expired, later citing the team's damaging actions in 1994 as his reason for opting out of his deal. A year later Benetton employees Rory Byrne (designer) and Ross Brawn (Technical Director) also joined Ferrari.

Ferrari had previously come close to winning the championship during 1982 then 1990 but the team had had a disastrous downturn in the early '90s, partly because its famous V12 engine was no longer competitive against the smaller, lighter, more fuel efficient V10s of its competitors. Alain Prost, among other drivers, had given the Ferraris labels including "truck", "pig", and "accident waiting to happen", with the poor performance of the Ferrari pit crews being regarded as a running joke. At the end of 1995, although the team had improved into a solid competitor, it was still considered inferior to front-running teams, including Benetton and Williams but Michael declared the Ferrari 412T good enough to win the Championship.

Schumacher, Ross Brawn, Rory Byrne, and Jean Todt, who joined in 1993, have been credited for turning the once struggling Ferrari team into the most successful one in Formula One history, 3-time World Champion Jackie Stewart believing that its transformation was Michael's greatest feat. Eddie Irvine was also recruited, moving from Jordan. During testing in the winter of 1995, Schumacher first drove their Ferrari 412 T2, being 2 secs faster than former regulars Jean Alesi and Gerhard Berger had been.

"It wasn't a race. It was a demonstration of brilliance."

Stirling Moss on Michael Schumacher at the Spanish Grand Prix of 1996

Michael finished third in the Drivers' Championship of 1996, helping Ferrari to become runners-up in the Constructors' Championship, ahead of his old team Benetton, winning 3 races, more than the team's total for the period from 1991 to 1995. Early in the season the car had reliability trouble, so Schumacher didn't finish 6 of the 16 races, but had his first win for Ferrari at the Spanish Grand Prix, where he lapped the entire field up to third place in the wet.

Having taken the lead on lap 19, he consistently lapped 5 secs faster than the rest of the field in the difficult conditions. In the French Grand Prix Michael qualified in pole position, but suffered engine failure on the race's formation lap. However, at Spa-Francorchamps, Schumacher used well-timed pit-stops to fend off Williams's Jacques Villeneuve, following which he won in front of the tifosi at Monza.

Michael vied for the title with Jacques during 1997, Villeneuve, driving the superior Williams FW19, having led the championship in the early part of the season. However, Schumacher had taken the championship lead by mid-season, winning 5 races to enter its final Grand Prix a point in front. Towards the end of the race, held at Jerez, Michael's Ferrari developed a coolant leak, reducing its performance, suggesting that he might not finish the race. As Jacques approached to overtake, Schumacher apparently tried to cause a collision, but came off worst then retired from the race, Villeneuve going on to take 4 points to win the championship. Michael was punished for unsportsmanlike conduct, being disqualified from the Drivers' Championship.

Finnish driver Mika Häkkinen became Schumacher's main competition for the title in 1998, Häkkinen winning the first 2 races of the season, to take a 16-point lead over Michael. Schumacher then won in Argentina, with the Ferrari improving significantly in the 2nd half of the season, Michael having 6 victories along with 5 other podium finishes. Ferrari had a 1–2 finish at the French Grand Prix, their first since 1990, with another at the Italian Grand Prix, which tied Schumacher with Mika for the Drivers' Championship lead with 80 points, but Häkkinen took the title by winning the final two races.

Michael was leading on the last lap of the British Grand Prix when he turned into the pit lane, crossed the start / finish line then stopped for a 10-secs stop go penalty. There was some doubt whether this counted as serving the penalty, but because he'd crossed the finish line when he came into the pit lane, the win was validated. At Spa, Schumacher was leading the race by 40 secs in heavy spray, but collided with David Coulthard's McLaren when the Scot, a lap down, slowed in very poor visibility to let Michael past. After both cars returned to the pits, Schumacher leaped out of his car then headed to McLaren's garage in an infuriated manner, accusing Coulthard of trying to kill him, David stating 5 years later that the accident had been his mistake.

Michael's efforts helped Ferrari to win the Constructors' title of 1999 but he lost his chance to win the Drivers' Championship at the British Grand Prix at the high-speed Stowe Corner, his car's rear brake failing, sending him off the track, resulting in a broken leg. During his 98-day absence, he was replaced by Finnish driver Mika Salo. After missing 6 races Schumacher made his return at the inaugural Malaysian Grand Prix, qualifying in pole position by almost a second. He then assumed the role of 2nd driver, supporting teammate Eddie Irvine's bid to win the Drivers' Championship for Ferrari. In the last race of the season, the Japanese Grand Prix, Häkkinen won his 2nd successive title, Michael later saying that he was the opponent that he respected the most.

During the period from 2000–2004 Schumacher won more races and championships than any other driver in the history of the sport. He won his third World Championship in the year 2000, after a year-long battle with Häkkinen. Michael won the first 3 races of the season, taking 5 of the first 8. Midway through the year his chances of lifting the title were reduced by 3 successive retirements, allowing Mika to close the gap in the standings, Häkkinen then winning 2 more races, before Schumacher triumphed at the Italian Grand Prix.

At the post race press conference, having equalled the number of victories (41) of his idol, Ayrton Senna, Michael broke down into tears. The outcome of the championship went down to the penultimate race of the season, the Japanese Grand Prix. Starting from pole position, Schumacher lost the lead to Mika at the start but after his 2nd pit-stop he came out ahead of Häkkinen, going on to win the race to lift his 3rd championship.

Michael took his 4th drivers' title during 2001, 4 other drivers winning races, but none sustaining a season-long challenge for the championship. Schumacher had a record-tying 9 wins, clinching the World Championship with 4 races to go, finishing with 123 points, 58 ahead of runner-up David Coulthard. At the Canadian Grand Prix, Michael finished 2nd to his brother Ralf, the first ever 1–2 finish by brothers in Formula One. At the Belgian Grand Prix Schumacher had his 52nd career win, breaking Alain Prost's record for most career wins.

Michael drove the Ferrari F2002 to retain his Drivers' Championship in 2002. However, there was again controversy at the Austrian Grand Prix, where his teammate, Rubens Barrichello was leading, but following team orders, slowed down to allow Schumacher to win over the final metres of the race. The crowd broke into outraged boos at the result, although Michael allowed Barrichello to stand on the top step of the podium.

At the US Grand Prix later that year, Schumacher dominated the race before slowing down intending to create a formation finish with Rubens, but slowed too much at the end allowing Barrichello to take the victory. In winning the Drivers' Championship Michael equalled the record set by Juan Manuel Fangio of 5 World Championships. Ferrari won 15 out of 17 races, Schumacher taking the title with 6 races left that season, which remains the earliest point in the season for a driver to be crowned World Champion. Michael broke his own record, shared with Nigel Mansell, of 9 race wins in a season, by winning 11 times, finishing every race on the podium. He finished with 144 points, a record-breaking 67 points ahead of the runner-up, his teammate Barrichello, the pair finishing 9 of the 17 races in the first two places.

Schumacher broke Fangio's record by winning the drivers' title for the 6th time during 2003, a closely contested season, his greatest competition again coming from the McLaren Mercedes and Williams BMW teams. Michael ran off track in the first race then in the following 2, was involved in collisions, falling 16 points behind Kimi Räikkönen but won the San Marino Grand Prix then the next two races, to close within 2 points of Räikkönen.

Apart from Schumacher's victory in Canada then Barrichello's win in Britain, the mid-season was dominated by Williams drivers Ralf Schumacher and Juan Pablo Montoya, who each had 2 victories. After the Hungarian Grand Prix, Michael led Montoya and Kimi by only one and 2 points, respectively.

Before the next race, the FIA announced changes to the way tyre widths were to be measured, forcing Michelin, supplier to Williams and McLaren among others, to rapidly redesign their tyres before the Italian Grand Prix.

Schumacher, running on Bridgestone tyres, won the next two races, so after Montoya was penalised in the US Grand Prix, only Michael and Räikkönen remained in contention for the title. At the final race, the Japanese Grand Prix, Schumacher needed only a point whilst Kimi needed to win, Michael taking the point he needed by finishing in 8th place to lift his 6th World Drivers' title, ending the season 2 points ahead of Räikkönen.

Schumacher won a record 12 of the first 13 races of the season in 2004, only failing to finish in Monaco after an accident with Juan Pablo Montoya during a safety car period, when he briefly locked his car's brakes. Michael clinched a record extending 7th drivers' title at the Belgian Grand Prix, ending the season with a record 148 points, 34 points ahead of the runner-up, his teammate Barrichello, also setting a new record of 13 race wins out of a possible 18, surpassing his previous best of 11 wins during the season of 2002.

Rule changes for the season of 2005 required tyres to last for an entire race, handing the overall advantage to teams using Michelins over teams including Ferrari that relied on Bridgestone tyres, partly being aimed at reducing Ferrari's dominance to make the races more interesting. Early in the season Schumacher battled with Fernando Alonso in San Marino, where he started 13th but finished only 0.2 seconds behind the Spaniard.

Under halfway through the season, Michael said "I don't think I can count myself in this battle any more. It was like trying to fight with a blunted weapon.... If your weapons are weak you don't have a chance." Schumacher's sole win of 2005 came at the US Grand Prix, before which the Michelin tyres were found to have significant safety issues. When no compromise between the teams and the FIA could be reached, all but the 6 drivers using Bridgestone tyres dropped out of the race after the formation lap. Michael retired in 6 of the 19 races, finishing the season in third with 62 points, less than half as many as World Champion Alonso.

The last season of Schumacher's Ferrari career came in 2006, when after 3 races, he had just 11 points, already being 17 points behind Fernando. Michael won the following two races, his pole position at San Marino having been his 66th, breaking Ayrton Senna's 12-year-old record. Schumacher was stripped of pole position at the Monaco Grand Prix, starting the race at the back of the grid, due to having stopped his car, blocking part of the circuit while Alonso was on his qualifying lap but he still managed to work his way up to 5th place on the notoriously cramped Monaco circuit.

By the Canadian Grand Prix, the 9th race of the season, Michael was 25 points behind Fernando, but then won the following 3 races to reduce his defecit to 11. After his victories in Italy, where Alonso had an engine failure then China, in which Fernando had tyre problems, Schumacher led the championship standings for the first time during the season. Although he and Alonso had the same points total, Michael was in front because he'd won more races.

The Japanese Grand Prix was led by Schumacher with only 16 laps to go, when, for the first time since the French Grand Prix of the year 2000, his car's engine failed, Fernando winning the race, to take a 10-point lead in the championship. With only one race left in the season, Michael could only lift the title if he won while Alonso got no points but before the Brazilian Grand Prix, Schumacher conceded the title to Alonso.

In pre-race ceremonies, footballing legend Pelé presented a trophy to Michael for his years of dedication to Formula One. During the race's qualifying, Schumacher had one of the quickest times during the first session then was fastest in the 2nd session but a fuel pressure problem prevented him from completing a single lap during the third session, so started the race in 10th position.

Early in the race Michael moved up to 6th place but in overtaking Fernando's teammate, Giancarlo Fisichella, his car had a tyre puncture caused by the front wing of Fisichella's car. Schumacher pitted, falling back to 19th place, 70 secs behind his teammate and race leader Felipe Massa but recovered, overtaking both Fisichella and Räikkönen to finish in 4th place. His performance was praised in the press as "heroic", an "utterly breath-taking drive", and a "performance that ... sums up his career".

While Michael was on the podium after winning the Italian Grand Prix of 2006, Ferrari issued a press release stating that he'd be retiring from racing at the end of that season, Schumacher confirming his retirement. The press issue stated that Michael would continue working for Ferrari, it being revealed on 29th October 2006 that Ferrari wanted him to be the assistant of their newly appointed CEO Jean Todt, involving selecting the team's future drivers.

Following Schumacher's confirmation of his retirement, leading Formula One figures including Niki Lauda and David Coulthard hailed Michael as the greatest all-round racing driver in the history of Formula One. The tifosi and the Italian press, who hadn't always taken to Schumacher's relatively cold public persona, also gave an affectionate response.

Michael attended several Grands Prix during the following season, having driven the Ferrari F2007 for the first time on 24th October at Ferrari's home track in Fiorano, Italy, completing only 5 laps, with no lap times being recorded. A Ferrari spokesman said the short drive was for the Fiat board of directors who were holding their meeting in Maranello.

Schumacher acted as Ferrari's adviser and Jean Todt's 'super assistant' during the 2007 season. Michael, who hadn't driven a Formula One car since he'd retired a year earlier, had a formal test session for the first time in the F2007 on 13th November that year. He returned the following month to continue helping Ferrari with their development programme at the Jerez circuit, focusing on testing electronics and tyres for the Formula One season of 2008.

Former Ferrari top manager Ross Brawn said in 2007 that Michael was very likely to be happy with continuing testing the following year, who later said that he'd "deal with the development of the car inside Gestione Sportiva", as part of which "I'd like to drive, but not too often". Schumacher also competed in motorcycle racing in the IDM Superbike-series during 2008, but stated that he'd no intention of having a 2nd competitive career in the sport. He was quoted as saying that riding a Ducati was the most exhilarating thing he'd done in his life, the 2nd most exciting being sky diving.

In his capacity as racing advisor to Ferrari, Michael was present in Budapest for the Hungarian Grand Prix when their driver

Felipe Massa was seriously injured after being struck by a suspension spring during qualifying. As it became clear that Massa wouldn't be able to compete in their next race at Valencia, Schumacher was chosen as a replacement for the Brazilian driver, Ferrari announcing on 29th July 2009 that they planned to draft him in for the European Grand Prix along with following races until Massa was able to compete again.

Michael tested in a modified F2007 to prepare himself, as he'd been unable to test the 2009 car due to testing restrictions. Ferrari appealed for special permission for Schumacher to test in a 2009 spec car, but Williams, Red Bull and Toro Rosso were against this. Michael then had to call off his return due to the severity of the neck injury that he'd received in a motorbike accident earlier that year, so Massa's place at Ferrari was filled by Luca Badoer and Giancarlo Fisichella instead. The Ferrari Museum in Maranello, Italy stated that it was planning an exhibition that would start on Schumacher's birthday then span a few months "both as a celebration and a mark of gratitude to the most successful Prancing Horse driver ever".

It was announced during December 2009 that Michael would be returning to Formula One the following season, alongside fellow German driver Nico Rosberg in the new Mercedes GP team, their first majority involvement in a F1 team since 1955. Schumacher stated that his preparations to replace the injured Massa for Ferrari had sparked a renewed interest in F1, which combined with the chance to fulfil a long-held ambition to drive for Mercedes and to work again with team principal Ross Brawn, had led him to accept their offer once he was passed fit.

Following a period of intensive training medical tests, it was confirmed that the neck injury that had stopped him driving for Ferrari the year before had fully healed, Schumacher signing a 3-year contract, reportedly worth £20m. Michael's surprise return to F1 was compared to Niki Lauda's in 1982 when aged 33 and Nigel Mansell's return during 1994 at the age of 41. Schumacher turned 41 in January 2010, his prospects with Mercedes being compared with the record set by the oldest F1 champion Juan Manuel Fangio, who was 46 when he won his 5th championship.

Michael's first drive of the Mercedes car for 2010– the Mercedes MGP W01 – was at an official test during February that year in Valencia then he finished 6th in the first race of the season at the Bahrain Grand Prix. After the Malaysian race, former driver Stirling Moss suggested that Schumacher, who'd finished behind his teammate in each of the first 4 qualifying sessions and races, might be "past it".

However, many other respected former Formula One drivers thought otherwise, including Michael's former rival Damon Hill, who warned "you should never write Schumacher off". GrandPrix.com identified the inherent understeer of the Mercedes car, exacerbated by the narrower front tyres introduced for that season, as contributing to Michael's difficulties. Jenson Button later stated that Mercedes's 2010 car was designed for him, suggesting that their differing driving styles may've contributed to Schumacher's problems.

Mercedes upgraded their car for the Spanish Grand Prix where Michael finished 4th then at the Monaco Grand Prix he finished 6th, after overtaking Ferrari's Fernando Alonso on the final corner of the race when the safety car returned to the pits.

However, Schumacher was penalised 20 secs after the race by the stewards, dropping him to 12th, who judged the passing manoevre to be in breach of the FIA's sporting code. Mercedes's differing interpretation of the regulation later led to it being clarified by the FIA.

Michael qualified 5th in Turkey, finishing 4th in the race, both his best results since his return but at the European Grand Prix in Valencia, he finished 15th, the lowest finish of his career. In Hungary, Schumacher finished outside the points in 11th, but was found guilty of dangerous driving at 180 mph, while unsuccessfully defending 10th position against Rubens Barrichello. This led to his demotion by 10 places on the grid for the following race, the Belgian Grand Prix, where he finished 7th, despite starting 21st after his grid penalty.

At the season finale in Abu Dhabi, Michael was involved in a major accident on the first lap, which took place after a spin. In recovering from the incident Vitantonio Liuzzi's car collided with Schumacher, barely missing his head, nobody being hurt in the crash, which he said had been "frightening". Michael finished the season 9th with 72 points, without having had a win, pole position, podium or fastest lap for the first time since his début during 1991.

Schumacher's first points of 2011 were in Malaysia, later coming 6th in Spain then having a strong race at the Canadian Grand Prix finishing 4th, after being as high as 2nd in a wet race. Michael was passed late in the race by the eventual winner Jenson Button. Schumacher clashed with Vitaly Petrov in Valencia then with Kamui Kobayashi in Britain, having marked the 20th anniversary of his Formula One début at the Belgian Grand Prix.

Despite starting last in Belgium, Michael raced well, finishing 5th, again doing well in Italy, duelling with Lewis Hamilton for 4th place. At the Japanese Grand Prix Schumacher led for 3 laps during the race, the first time he'd led a race since 2006, becoming the oldest driver to lead a race since Jack Brabham in 1970. At the Indian Grand Prix Michael started well, finishing 5th after overtaking Nico Rosberg at the end of the race. Schumacher battled over 6th position on the first lap with Nico at the Abu Dhabi Grand Prix, before finishing the season in 8th place in the Drivers' Championship, with 76 points.

Michael was again partnered by Rosberg at Mercedes for the season of 2012, retiring from the first race of the season at the Australian Grand Prix then taking just a point in the 2nd round in Malaysia. In China Schumacher started on the front row alongside Nico on pole, but retired due to a loose wheel after a mechanic's error during a pit stop. After causing a collision with Bruno Senna in Spain, Michael received a 5-place grid penalty for the Monaco Grand Prix, where he was fastest in qualifying but started 6th, later retiring from 7th place in the race.

At the European Grand Prix, Schumacher finished 3rd in the race, his only podium finish since his return to F1 with Mercedes. At the age of 43 years and 173 days, he became the oldest driver to make the podium since Jack Brabham's 2nd-place finish at the British Grand Prix of 1970. More records were set by Michael in Germany, where he set the fastest lap in a Grand Prix for the 77th time in his career then in Belgium where he became the 2nd driver in history to have raced in 300 Grands Prix.

Schumacher's indecision over his future plans in F1 then led to him being replaced by Lewis Hamilton at Mercedes for the season of 2013, so he announced during October 2012 that he'd retire for the 2nd time at the end of the season. The following week Michael was quoted as saying: "There were times over the past few months when I didn't want to deal with Formula One or prepare for the next Grand Prix." The season and his 21-year F1 career concluded with the Brazilian Grand Prix of 2012, in which Schumacher finished 7th, having come 13th in that year's Drivers' Championship.

Michael, in conjunction with Schuberth, helped develop the first lightweight carbon helmet in 2004, a prototype being publicly tested by being driven over by a tank, which it survived intact. The helmet kept the driver cool by funneling directed airflow through 50 holes, Schumacher's original helmet displaying the colours of the German flag, along with his sponsor's decals, a blue circle with white astroids being on top.

To differentiate his colours from his new teammate Rubens Barrichello, Michael changed the upper blue colour and some of the white areas to red, from the Monaco Grand Prix of the year 2000. Schumacher wore an all-red helmet that included the names of his 91 Grand Prix victories for the Brazilian Grand Prix race of 2006, at the time intended to be his final Grand Prix.

He wore a commemorative gold-leafed helmet for the Belgian Grand Prix of 2011, Michael's 20th anniversary in Formula One. The helmet, very similar to his latest helmet, included the year of his début to 2011, with the years of his 7 World titles. For the

Belgian Grand Prix of 2012, Schumacher's 300th Grand Prix appearance, he wore a special platinum-leafed helmet with a message of his achievement.

Honours

Michael was named as one of the UNESCO Champions for sport during April 2002 for his contributions to sport and to raising awareness of child education, joining the other 8, which included Pelé, Sergey Bubka and Justine Henin. Schumacher won the Laureus World Sportsman of the Year award twice, in 2002 & 2004, for his performances during the 2001 & 2003 seasons respectively, having also received nominations for the 2001, 2003, 2005 and 2007 awards.

Michael shares the record for having the 2nd-most nominations for the award with Roger Federer with 6 nominations, being eclipsed only by Tiger Woods, who's been nominated 7 times. Schumacher has had the most nominations for a motorsport athlete, Fernando Alonso having been nominated twice, Sebastian Vettel 3 times, and Valentino Rossi 5 times, being the only motorsport athlete to have won the award more than once.

Michael was awarded an FIA Gold Medal for Motor Sport in 2006, in honour of his racing career and his efforts to improve safety and the sport. In recognition of his contribution to Formula One racing, the Nürburgring race track renamed turns 8 and 9, the Audi and Shell Kurves, as the Schumacher S the following year. A month later he presented A1 Team Germany with the A1 World Cup at the A1GP World Cup of Motorsport awards ceremony of 2007. Michael was nominated for the Prince of Asturias Award for Sport for that year, which he won both for sporting prowess and for his humanitarian record.

The Swiss Football Association appointed long-time Swiss resident Schumacher as the country's ambassador for the European football championships of 2008. Michael was honoured with the Officier of Légion d'honneur title by French prime minister François Fillon on 30th April 2010. Schumacher was awarded the Millennium Trophy at the Bambi Awards on 13th November 2014.

Going into the Australian Grand Prix of 1994, the final race of that season, Michael led Damon Hill by a single point in the Drivers' Championship. He led the race from the start, but on lap 35 he went off track, hitting the wall with his right side wheels, returning to the track at reduced speed, with a damaged car, but still leading the race. At the next corner Hill tried to pass on the inside but Schumacher turned in sharply, so they collided. Both cars were eliminated from the race, neither driver scoring, so Michael took the title. The race stewards judged it a racing accident, having taken no action against either driver, but public opinion was divided over the incident, Schumacher being vilified in the British media.

At the European Grand Prix at Jerez, the last race of the season of 1997, Michael led Williams's Jacques Villeneuve by just a point in the Drivers' Championship. As Villeneuve tried to pass Schumacher at the Dry Sac corner on lap 48, Michael turned in so the right-front wheel of his Ferrari hit the left sidepod of Jacques's car, Schumacher having to retire from the race, but

Villeneuve finishing in third place, taking 4 points to become the World Champion.

The race stewards didn't award any penalty at first, but a fortnight after the race Michael was disqualified from the entire Drivers' Championship of 1997, after an FIA disciplinary hearing decided that his "manoeuvre was an instinctive reaction and although deliberate wasn't made with malice or premeditation. It was a serious error." Schumacher accepted the decision, admitting having made a mistake, his actions being widely condemned in British, German, and Italian newspapers. Michael remains the only driver in the history of the sport to have been disqualified from a Drivers' World Championship.

Historically, team orders have always been an accepted part of Formula One but in the final metres of the Austrian Grand Prix of 2002, Schumacher's teammate, Rubens Barrichello, slowed his car under orders from Ferrari to allow Michael to pass to win the race. Although this didn't break any regulation, it angered many fans, who thought that the team's actions showed a lack of sportsmanship and respect to the spectators.

It was argued that Schumacher didn't need to be "given" wins in only the 6th race of the season, particularly given that he'd already won 4 of the previous 5 Grands Prix, and that Barrichello had dominated the race weekend up to that point. At the podium ceremony, Michael pushed Rubens onto the top step, for which the Ferrari team were fined US$1 million.

Later that season at the end of the United States Grand Prix, Schumacher slowed down within sight of the finishing line, allowing Barrichello to win by 0.011 seconds, the 2nd closest margin in F1 history. Michael's explanation varied between it being him "returning the favour" for Austria, Schumacher's title having already been secured, or trying to engineer a dead-heat, a feat derided as near-impossible in a sport where timings are taken to within a thousandth of a second. The FIA subsequently banned "team orders which interfere with the race result", but it was lifted for the 2011 season because the ruling was difficult to enforce.

During his spell in Sauber, in the Sportscar World Championship of 1991, Michael was involved in a serious incident with Derek Warwick in that year's 430 km of Nürburgring. While trying to set his flying lap in qualifying, Schumacher encountered Warwick's Jaguar on a slow lap, holding him up. As retaliation for being in his way, Michael swerved his Sauber into Warwick's car, hitting the Jaguar's nose and front wheel. Enraged by the German's actions, Derek drove to the pits then chased a fleeing Schumacher on foot through the Sauber pits, catching him up, it taking an intervention from Jochen Mass to stop Warwick from physically assaulting Michael.

Toward the end of the Hungarian Grand Prix of 2010, Rubens Barrichello tried to pass Schumacher down the inside on the main straight. Michael closed the inside line to force Barrichello onto the outside, but Rubens persisted on the inside at 180 mph, despite the close proximity of a concrete wall, Schumacher leaving him only inches to spare. Barrichello said "It is the most dangerous thing that I've been through. There's not a rule for that but between ourselves we should take a line, stick to it and that's it."

Michael said that "Obviously there was space enough to go through. We didn't touch, so I guess I just left enough space for him to come through." Ross Brawn said "at the end of the day he gave him enough space. You can argue that it was marginal, but it was just tough – tough racing." However, a range of ex-drivers and commentators were highly critical of Schumacher.

Although there was no accident, the race steward, Derek Warwick of the 1991 Nürburgring incident, wanted to black flag Michael as that "would've shown a better example to our young drivers". The Hungaroring incident was ruled to be dangerous, Schumacher receiving a 10 place grid penalty for the next race, having accepted the decision then apologised.

Suspicion of foul play by the Benetton team during 1994, who were later found to have been responsible for some technical violations over the course of the season, was said to have troubled Ayrton Senna that year. In the words of his then teammate, Damon Hill, Senna had chosen to stay at the first corner of the Aida circuit following his retirement from the Pacific Grand Prix.

After listening to Michael's Benetton B194 as it went past, Senna "concluded that there were what he regarded as unusual noises from the engine". The FIA later issued a press release setting out action that it required teams to take before the German Grand Prix, given that some cars were found to have advanced engine management systems, emulating launch and traction control.

Schumacher and Williams driver David Coulthard were disqualified for fuel irregularities in 1995, after a switch to Renault engines and Elf oils. On appeal, both drivers had their results and points reinstated, but both teams lost the points that the results would normally have earned in the Constructors' Championship. During the Canadian Grand Prix of 1998 Michael was accused of dangerous driving, when his exit from the pit-lane forced Heinz-Harald Frentzen off the track and into retirement. Despite receiving a 10-sec penalty, Schumacher recovered to win the race.

Two laps from the end of the British Grand Prix of 1998, Michael was leading the race when he was issued a stop go penalty for overtaking the lapped car of Alexander Wurz during the early moments of a Safety Car period. This penalty involves going into the pit lane then stopping for 10 secs, the rules stating that a driver must serve his penalty within 3 laps of the penalty being issued.

On the third lap after receiving the penalty, Schumacher turned into the pit lane to serve his penalty, but as it was the last lap of the race, with Ferrari's pit box being located beyond the start/finish line, Michael technically finished the race before serving the penalty. The stewards initially resolved the problem by adding 10 secs to Schumacher's race time but later rescinded the penalty completely due to irregularities in how the penalty had been issued.

During qualifying for the Monaco Grand Prix of 2006, Michael set the fastest time but his car stopped in the Rascasse corner on the racing line, leaving the corner partially blocked, while his main contender for that season's title, Fernando Alonso, was on his final qualifying lap. Schumacher stated that he simply locked up the wheels going into the corner, the car then stalling while he tried to reverse out.

Alonso believed that he'd have been on pole if the incident hadn't happened, Michael being stripped of pole position by the race stewards, starting the race from the back of the grid. In the same qualifying session, Giancarlo Fisichella was similarly found to have blocked David Coulthard from improving his time, but Fisichella was only demoted 5 places on the grid.

At the Monaco Grand Prix of 2010, the safety car was deployed after an accident involving Karun Chandhok and Jarno Trulli then pulled into the pits on the last lap, Schumacher passing Alonso before the finish line. Mercedes held that "the combination of the race control messages 'Safety Car in this lap' and 'Track Clear' and the green flags and lights shown by the marshals after safety car line one, indicated that the race wasn't finishing under the safety car, so all drivers were free to race." However, an FIA investigation found Michael guilty of breaching Safety Car regulations, handing him a 20-secs penalty, which cost him 6 places.

Schumacher's younger brother Ralf was also a racing driver, who competed in Formula One for 10 years, from 1997 until the end of 2007. Their step-brother Sebastian Stahl has also been a racing driver. Michael wed Corinna Betsch during August 1995, the couple having 2 children, a daughter Gina-Marie, born 20th February 1997 then a son Mick, born 22nd March 1999.

Schumacher has always been very protective of his private life, having been known to dislike the celebrity spotlight. The family moved to a newly-built mansion near Gland, Switzerland in 2007, covering an area of 7,000 sq ft, with a private beach on Lake Geneva, featuring an underground garage and petrol station. Michael's son Mick was announced as a driver for the Ferrari Driver Academy on 19th January 2019.

Schumacher and his wife own horse ranches in Texas and Switzerland. The family has two dogs – a stray that Corinna fell in love with in Brazil, and an Australian Shepherd named "Ed" whose arrival in the family made headlines. Michael drove a taxi through the Bavarian town of Coburg to collect the dog during 2007, enabling the family to make their return flight to Switzerland, both Schumacher and the taxi driver being reprimanded by local police.

One of Michael's main hobbies was horse riding, having also played football for his local team FC Echichens. He's appeared in several charity football games and organised games between Formula One drivers. Schumacher was appointed as an Ambassador-at-Large for the Most Serene Republic of San Marino on 23rd June 2003.

Michael was made a special ambassador to UNESCO, having donated 1.5 million euros to the organization. He's also paid for the construction of a school for poor children and for area improvements in Dakar, Senegal. Schumacher supports a hospital for child victims of war in Sarajevo, which specialises in caring for amputees. In Lima, Peru he funded the "Palace for the Poor", a centre for helping homeless street children get an education, clothing, food, medical attention, and shelter. Michael stated that his interest in these efforts was piqued both by his love for children and the fact that the causes had received little attention. In his last 4 years as a driver, he donated at least $50 million, it having been revealed in 2008 that he'd donated between $5M and $10M to the Clinton Foundation.

Following his participation in an FIA European road safety campaign, as part of his punishment after the collision at the

European Grand Prix during 1997, Schumacher continued to support other campaigns. These included Make Roads Safe, led by the FIA Foundation, which calls on G8 countries and the UN to recognise global road deaths as a major global health issue.

Michael was the figurehead of an ad campaign by Bacardi in 2008, to raise awareness about responsible drinking, with a focus on communicating the international message 'drinking and driving don't mix'. He featured in an ad campaign on TV, cinema and online media, supported by consumer engagements, public relations and digital media across the World. On the eve of the British Grand Prix of 2002, Schumacher presented a Ferrari 360 Modena to the Indian cricketer Sachin Tendulkar at Silverstone, on behalf of Fiat.

Michael appeared on the BBC2 TV motoring programme Top Gear as the Stig on 21st June 2009. Presenter Jeremy Clarkson hinted later in the programme that Schumacher wasn't the regular Stig, which the BBC subsequently confirmed. Michael was there on that occasion because Ferrari wouldn't allow anyone else to drive the unique black Ferrari FXX that was featured in the show. During his interview with Clarkson, Schumacher stated that his road cars were a Fiat 500 Abarth, and a Fiat Croma, which was his family car.

Forbes magazine listed him as the 2nd highest paid sportsman in the world during 2004 then Eurobusiness magazine stated that Michael was the world's first billionaire athlete the following year, his salary having been reported as c. US$80 million. Forbes magazine ranked Schumacher 17th in its "The World's Most Powerful Celebrities" list. A significant part of his income came from advertising, Deutsche Vermögensberatung having paid him $8 million over 3 years from 1999 for wearing a

10 by 8 cm ad on his post-race cap, the deal being extended until 2010.

Michael donated $10 million for aid after the Indian Ocean earthquake of 2004, his donation having exceeded that of any other sports person, most sports leagues, many worldwide corporations and some countries. Schumacher's bodyguard Burkhard Cramer and Cramer's two sons were killed in the tsunami. Michael's personal fortune was estimated at £515 million in 2010, having reportedly received a salary of £21 million / year from the Mercedes team, plus a further £9 million in endorsements.

Schumacher was skiing with his 14-year-old son Mick on 29th December 2013, descending the Combe de Saulire below the Dent de Burgin above Méribel in the French Alps. While crossing an unsecured off-piste area between Piste Chamois and Piste Mauduit, Michael fell, hitting his head on a rock, sustaining a serious head injury despite wearing a ski helmet. His doctors stated that he'd probably have died if he hadn't been wearing a helmet.

Schumacher was airlifted to Grenoble Hospital where he was operated on twice then put into a medically induced coma, because of traumatic brain injury; his doctors stating on 7th March 2014 that his condition was stable. Michael's agent said on 4th April that he had "moments of consciousness," as he was gradually withdrawn from the coma, following reports by relatives of "small encouraging signs" over the preceding month.

Schumacher was moved from intensive care into a rehabilitation ward during mid-June of that year, having regained consciousness then left Grenoble Hospital for further rehabilitation at the University Hospital (CHUV) in Lausanne, Switzerland on 16th June. Michael left CHUV on 9th September 2014, being taken back home for further rehabilitation. It was reported that November that Schumacher was "paralysed and in a wheelchair, cannot speak and has memory problems". In a video interview released in May 2015, Michael's manager Sabine Kehm said that his condition was slowly improving, "considering the severity of the injury he had".

Felix Damm, Schumacher's lawyer, told a German court during September 2016 that his client "cannot walk", in response to false reports the previous December in the German publication, Die Bunte that he could "walk a couple of steps". Michael's manager stated in December 2016 that "Michael's health is not a public issue, so we'll continue to make no comment in that regard".

Former Ferrari manager, Jean Todt, gave an interview to Radio Monte Carlo during July 2019, giving a brief update on Schumacher's health, saying that he was making "good progress" but "struggles to communicate". Todt also said that Michael was able to watch Formula One races on TV at his home in Switzerland.

Racing record

Career summary

Season	Series	Team	Races	Wins	Poles	F/Laps	Podiums	Points	Position
1988	European Formula Ford 1600	Eufra Racing	4	1	1	0	3	50	2nd
	German Formula Ford 1600		7	3	0	0	5	124	6th
	Formula König	Hoecker Sportwagenservice	10	9	1	1	10	192	1st
1989	German Formula Three	WTS Racing	12	2	2	0	7	163	3rd
	European Formula Three Cup		1	0	0	0	0	N/A	NC
	Macau Grand Prix		1	0	0	0	0	N/A	NC
1990	World Sportscar Championship	Team Sauber Mercedes	3	1	0	1	3	21	5th
	German Formula Three	WTS Racing	11	5	6	4	7	148	1st
	European Formula Three Cup		1	0	1	1	0	N/A	NC
	Macau Grand Prix		1	1	0	0	0	N/A	1st
	Deutsche Tourenwagen Meisterschaft	HWA AG	1	0	0	0	0	0	NC

1991   Formula One   Team 7UP Jordan   1   0
0   0   0   0   14th

Camel Benetton Ford   5   0   0   0   0
4

World Sportscar Championship Team Sauber Mercedes 8
1   0   2   2   43   9th

Deutsche Tourenwagen Meisterschaft   Zakspeed Racing
4   0   0   0   0   0   NC

Japanese Formula 3000 Team LeMans   1   0   0
0   1   6   12th

1992   Formula One   Camel Benetton Ford   16   1
0   2   8   53   3rd

1993   Formula One   Camel Benetton Ford   16   1
0   5   9   52   4th

1994   Formula One   Mild Seven Benetton Ford   14
8   6   8   10   92   1st

1995   Formula One   Mild Seven Benetton Renault   17
9   4   8   11   102   1st

1996   Formula One   Scuderia Ferrari S.p.A.   16   3
4   2   8   59   3rd

1997   Formula One   Scuderia Ferrari Marlboro   17
5   3   3   8   78   DSQ

1998   Formula One   Scuderia Ferrari Marlboro   16   6
3   6   11   86   2nd

| 1999 | Formula One | Scuderia Ferrari Marlboro | 10 | 2 |
| 3 | 5 | 6 | 44 | 5th |

| 2000 | Formula One | Scuderia Ferrari Marlboro | 17 | 9 |
| 9 | 2 | 12 | 108 | 1st |

| 2001 | Formula One | Scuderia Ferrari Marlboro | 17 | 9 |
| 11 | 3 | 14 | 123 | 1st |

| 2002 | Formula One | Scuderia Ferrari Marlboro | 17 | 11 |
| 7 | 7 | 17 | 144 | 1st |

| 2003 | Formula One | Scuderia Ferrari Marlboro | 16 | 6 |
| 5 | 5 | 8 | 93 | 1st |

| 2004 | Formula One | Scuderia Ferrari Marlboro | 18 | 13 |
| 8 | 10 | 15 | 148 | 1st |

| 2005 | Formula One | Scuderia Ferrari Marlboro | 19 | |
| 1 | 1 | 3 | 5 | 62 | 3rd |

| 2006 | Formula One | Scuderia Ferrari Marlboro | 18 | 7 |
| 4 | 7 | 12 | 121 | 2nd |

| 2010 | Formula One | Mercedes GP Petronas F1 Team 19 |
| 0 | 0 | 0 | 0 | 72 | 9th |

| 2011 | Formula One | Mercedes GP Petronas F1 Team 19 |
| 0 | 0 | 0 | 0 | 76 | 8th |

| 2012 | Formula One | Mercedes AMG Petronas F1 Team |
| 20 | 0 | 0 | 1 | 1 | 49 | 13th |

Source: Hilton, Christopher (2006). Michael Schumacher: The Whole Story. Haynes. ISBN 1-84425-008-3.

Complete World Sportscar Championship results

Year	Entrant	Class	Chassis	Engine	1	2
3	4	5	6	7	8	9
Pos.	Pts					

1990	Team Sauber Mercedes	C		Mercedes-Benz C11		
Mercedes-Benz M119 5.0 V8t		SUZ		MNZ		SIL
DNQ	SPA	DIJ 2	NÜR 2	DON	CGV	MEX 1	5th
21						

1991	Team Sauber Mercedes	C1		Mercedes-Benz C291		
Mercedes-Benz M291 3.5 F12		SUZ Ret	MNZ	Ret		
SIL 2	NÜR Ret	MAG Ret		MEX Ret	AUT 1	
9th	43					

C2	Mercedes-Benz C11		Mercedes-Benz M119 5.0 V8t	
LMS 5				

Complete Deutsche Tourenwagen Meisterschaft results

Year	Team	Car	1	2	3	4	5
6	7	8	9	10	11	12
13	14	15	16	17	18	19
20	21	22	23	24	Pos.	Pts

1990	AMG Motorenbau GmbH		Mercedes 190 E 2.5-16
Evo II	ZOL		

1	ZOL 2	HOC 1	HOC 2	NÜR 1	NÜR 2	AVU 1	AVU 2
MFA 1	MFA 2	WUN 1	WUN 2	NÜR 1	NÜR 2	NOR 1
NOR 2	DIE 1	DIE 2	NÜR 1	NÜR 2	HOC 1	Ret
HOC 2	DNS	NC	0			

1991   Zakspeed Racing   Mercedes 190 E 2.5-16 Evo II
ZOL

1	ZOL 2	HOC 1	HOC 2	NÜR 1	NÜR 2	AVU 1	AVU 2
	WUN 1	WUN 2	NOR 1	25	NOR 2	Ret	DIE 1
Ret	DIE 2 14		NÜR 1	NÜR 2	ALE 1	ALE 2	HOC 1
	HOC 2	BRN 1	BRN 2	DON 1	DON 2	NC	0

24 Hours of Le Mans results

Year	Team	Co-drivers	Car	Class	Laps	Pos.	Class pos.
1991	Team Sauber Mercedes	Karl Wendlinger Fritz Kreutzpointner	Mercedes-Benz C11	C2	355	5th	5th

Complete Japanese Formula 3000 Championship results

Year	Entrant	Chassis	Engine	1	2	3	4	5	6	7	8	9	10	11	Pos.	Pts
1991	Team LeMans	Ralt RT23	Mugen	SUZ	AUT	FUJ	MIN	SUZ	SUG 2	FUJ	SUZ	FUJ	SUZ	FUJ	12th	6

Complete Formula One results

Year	Entrant	Chassis	Engine	1	2	3	4	5	6	7	8	9	10

11   12   13   14   15   16   17
18   19   20   WDC   Pts

1991   Team 7UP Jordan   Jordan 191   Ford HBB 4 3.5
V8   USA   BRA   SMR   MON   CAN   MEX   FRA
        GBR   GER   HUN   BEL Ret   14th   4

Camel Benetton Ford   Benetton B191 Ford HBA 5 3.5 V8
          ITA 5   POR 6   ESP 6 JPN RetAUS Ret

1992 Camel Benetton Ford Benetton B191B Ford HB 3.5 V8
RSA 4   MEX 3   BRA 3   3rd   53

Benetton B192 ESP 2 SMR Ret   MON 4 CAN 2 FRA
Ret GBR 4   GER 3   HUN Ret   BEL 1   ITA 3   POR 7
JPN Ret   AUS 2

1993   Camel Benetton Ford   Benetton B193   Ford HB 3.5
V8   RSA Ret   BRA 3   4th   52

Benetton B193B EUR Ret SMR 2   ESP 3 MON Ret CAN 2
FRA 3 GBR 2 GER 2 HUN Ret BEL 2   ITA Ret POR 1 JPN Ret
          AUS Ret

1994   Mild Seven Benetton Ford   Benetton B194   Ford
Zetec-R 3.5 V8 BRA 1 PAC 1   SMR 1   MON 1 ESP 2 CAN 1
FRA 1 GBR DSQ   GER Ret HUN 1 BEL DSQ   ITA
          POR   EUR 1   JPN 2   AUS Ret   1st   92

1995   Mild Seven Benetton Renault   Benetton B195
Renault RS7 3.0 V10 BRA 1 ARG 3   SMR Ret ESP 1 MON
1 CAN 5 FRA 1   GBR Ret GER 1 HUN 11†   BEL 1
          ITA Ret POR 2   EUR 1   PAC 1 JPN 1 AUS Ret
          1st   102

88

1996   Scuderia Ferrari S.p.A.   Ferrari F310   Ferrari 046 3.0 V10   AUS Ret BRA 3   ARG Ret EUR 2 SMR 2 MON Ret   ESP 1   CAN Ret FRA DNS   GBR Ret GER 4 HUN 9†   BEL 1   ITA 1   POR 3   JPN 2   3rd   59

1997   Scuderia Ferrari Marlboro   Ferrari F310B   Ferrari 046/2 3.0 V10   AUS 2 BRA 5 ARG Ret   SMRT 2   MON 1 ESP 4 CAN 1   FRA GBR Ret   GER 2 HUN 4   BEL 1   ITA 6   AUT 6   LUX Ret JPN 1   EUR Ret   DSQ‡   78

1998   Scuderia Ferrari Marlboro   Ferrari F300   Ferrari 047 3.0 V10   AUS Ret BRA 3   ARG 1   SMR 2 ESP 3 MON 10   CAN 1   FRA 1   GBR 1 AUT 3 GER 5 HUN 1 BEL Ret ITA 1   LUX 2   JPN Ret   2nd   86

1999   Scuderia Ferrari Marlboro   Ferrari F399   Ferrari 048 3.0 V10   AUS 8   BRA 2 SMR 1   MON 1 ESP 3 CAN Ret   FRA 5   GBR DNS AUT GER   HUN BEL ITA EUR   MAL 2   JPN 2 5th   44

2000   Scuderia Ferrari Marlboro   Ferrari F1-2000 Ferrari 049 3.0 V10   AUS 1   BRA 1 SMR 1   GBR 3 ESP 5 EUR 1 MON Ret   CAN 1 FRA Ret AUT Ret GER Ret HUN 2 BEL 2   ITA 1   USA 1   JPN 1   MAL 1 1st   108

2001   Scuderia Ferrari Marlboro   Ferrari F2001   Ferrari 050 3.0 V10   AUS 1   MAL 1 BRA 2   SMR Ret ESP 1 AUT 2 MON 1 CAN 2   EUR 1   FRA 1   GBR 2   GER Ret   HUN 1   BEL 1   ITA 4   USA 2   JPN 1   1st   123

2002   Scuderia Ferrari Marlboro Ferrari F2001 Ferrari 050 3.0 V10. AUS 1 MAL 3

Ferrari F2002   Ferrari 051 3.0 V10   BRA 1   SMR 1   ESP 1
AUT 1   MON 2   CAN 1   EUR 2   GBR 1   FRA 1   GER 1   HUN 2
BEL 1   ITA 2   USA 2   JPN 1   1st   144

2003   Scuderia Ferrari Marlboro   Ferrari F2002   Ferrari
051 3.0 V10   AUS 4   MAL 6 BRA Ret   SMR 1

Ferrari F2003-GA   Ferrari 052 3.0 V10   ESP 1   AUT 1
MON 3   CAN 1   EUR 5   FRA 3   GBR 4   GER 7   HUN 8   ITA 1
USA 1   JPN 8   1st   93

2004   Scuderia Ferrari Marlboro   Ferrari F2004   Ferrari
053 3.0 V10   AUS 1   MAL 1 BHR 1   SMR 1   ESP 1   MON
Ret   EUR 1   CAN 1   USA 1   FRA 1 GBR 1   GER 1   HUN 1
        BEL 2   ITA 2   CHN 12   JPN 1   BRA 7 1st   148

2005   Scuderia Ferrari Marlboro   Ferrari F2004M   Ferrari
053 3.0 V10   AUS Ret   MAL 7

Ferrari F2005   Ferrari 055 3.0 V10   BHR Ret   SMR 2   ESP
Ret   MON 7   EUR 5   CAN 2 USA 1   FRA 3   GBR 6   GER 5
HUN 2   TUR Ret   ITA 10   BEL Ret   BRA 4   JPN 7   CHN
Ret   3rd   62

2006   Scuderia Ferrari Marlboro   Ferrari 248 F1   Ferrari
056 2.4 V8   BHR 2   MAL 6 AUS Ret   SMR 1   EUR 1   ESP 2
MON 5 GBR 2   CAN 2   USA 1   FRA 1   GER 1   HUN 8† TUR 3
ITA 1   CHN 1   JPN Ret   BRA 4   2nd   121

2010   Mercedes GP Petronas F1 Team Mercedes MGP W01
        Mercedes FO 108X 2.4 V8   BHR 6   AUS 10   MAL
Ret   CHN 10   ESP 4   MON 12   TUR 4   CAN 11   EUR 1
GBR 9   GER 9   HUN 11   BEL 7   ITA 9   SIN 13   JPN 6   KOR 4
BRA 7   ABU Ret   9th   72

2011   Mercedes GP Petronas F1 Team Mercedes MGP W02
        Mercedes FO 108Y 2.4 V8   AUS   Ret   MAL 9
        CHN 8   TUR 12   ESP 6   MON Ret   CAN 4   EUR
17 GBR 9 GER 8   HUN Ret   BEL 5   ITA 5   SIN Ret   JPN 6
KOR Ret   IND 5   ABU 7   BRA 15   8th   76

2012   Mercedes AMG Petronas F1 Team   Mercedes F1
W03   Mercedes FO 108Z 2.4 V8   AUS Ret   MAL 10
        CHN Ret   BHR 10 ESP Ret MON Ret   CAN
Ret   EUR 3   GBR 7   GER 7 HUN Ret   BEL 7   ITA 6
SIN Ret   JPN 11   KOR 13   IND 22†   ABU 11 USA 16 BRA 7
13th   49

‡ Schumacher was disqualified from the 1997 World Drivers'
Championship due to dangerous driving in the European Grand
Prix, where he caused an avoidable accident with Jacques
Villeneuve. His points tally would have placed him in 2nd place
in that year's standings.

† Driver did not finish the Grand Prix, but was classified as he
completed over 90% of the race distance.

Formula One records

Schumacher holds the following records in Formula One:

Record	Date first achieved	Current Record
Most Championship titles	2003	7
Most consecutive titles	2000–2004	5
Most races left in the season when becoming World Champion	2002	6

Most career wins   2001 Belgian Grand Prix 91

Most wins in a season   2004   13

Most wins with the same team 2002 Brazilian Grand Prix
        72

Most pole positions at the same Grand Prix   Japan 1994–
1995, 1998–2002, 2004 8

Most wins at the same Grand Prix France 1994–1995, 1997–
1998, 2001–2002, 2004, 2006   8

Most seasons with a win   1992–2006   15

Most consecutive seasons with a win   1992–2006   15

Most second places   2004 Italian Grand Prix   43

Most consecutive top two finishes   Brazil 2002–Japan 2002
        15

Most podium finishes   2002 British Grand Prix 155

Most podium finishes in a season   2002   17

Most consecutive podium finishes   2001 US Grand Prix–
2002 Japanese Grand Prix   19

Most races finished in the points   2002 Italian Grand Prix
        221

Most races led   2001 Belgian Grand Prix 142

Most laps led   2001 French Grand Prix 5,111

Longest distance led (km)   2001 French Grand Prix 24,148

Most fastest laps   2001 Australian Grand Prix   77

Most fastest laps in a season   2004   10

Most hat-tricks (pole, win and fastest lap)   2002 Japanese
Grand Prix   22

Most hat-tricks in a season   2004   5

Most races with a single constructor   2005 European Grand
Prix   181

Books and films

Allen, James (1999). Michael Schumacher: Driven to Extremes.
Bantam Books. ISBN 978-0-553-81214-5.

Allen, James (2007). Edge of Greatness. Headline. ISBN 978-0-
7553-1678-6.

Collings, Timothy (2004). The Piranha Club. Virgin Books. ISBN
978-0-7535-0965-4.

Collings, Timothy (2005). Team Schumacher. Highdown. ISBN
978-1-905156-03-0.

Domenjoz, Luc (2002). Michael Schumacher: Rise of a genius.
Parragon. ISBN 978-0-7525-9228-2.

Henry, Alan (ed.) (1992). Autocourse 1992–93. Hazleton
Publishing. ISBN 978-0-905138-96-1.

Henry, Alan (1996). Wheel to Wheel: Great Duels of Formula
One Racing. Weidenfeld Nicolson Illustrated. ISBN 978-0-7538-
0522-0.

Hilton, Christopher (2003). Michael Schumacher: The greatest of all. Haynes. ISBN 978-1-84425-044-8.

Hilton, Christopher (2006). Michael Schumacher: The Whole Story. Haynes. ISBN 978-1-84425-008-0.

Kehm, Sabine (2003). Michael Schumacher. Driving Force. Random House. ISBN 978-0-09-189435-1.

Matchett, Steve (1995). Life in the Fast Lane: The Story of the Benetton Grand Prix Year. London: Weidenfeld and Nicolson. ISBN 978-0-297-81610-2.

Matchett, Steve (1999). The Mechanic's Tale: Life in the Pit Lanes of Formula One. Osceola, Wisconsin: MBI Pub. ISBN 978-0-7603-0754-0.

Williams, Richard (1999). The Death of Ayrton Senna. Bloomsbury. ISBN 978-0-7475-4495-1.

Schumacher had a voice role in the Disney/Pixar film Cars. His character was himself as a Ferrari F430. The French movie Asterix and Obelix at the Olympic Games featured Schumacher in a cameo role as a chariot driver called Schumix.

CPSIA information can be obtained
at www.ICGtesting.com
Printed in the USA
LVHW010321091019
633651LV00011B/421/P